Reclaim Control of Your Life

> The Companion Workbook to
>
> *Change Course: One Lady's Race from Acceptance to Adventure*

Leslie Jackson

Reclaim Control of Your Life Copyright © 2020 Leslie Jackson

All Rights Reserved
Printed in the United States of America

No part of this book may be reproduced in any form or by any means, electronic or mechanical, including photography, recording, e-books, or any information storage and retrieval system, without permission in writing from the publisher.

ISBN: 978-1-7345854-2-1

Illustrations and Cover Design by Lacey Ballard
Interior Design by Sue Stein

For information:
www.LadyRacing.com
Leslie@LadyRacing.com

Table of Contents

Introduction: Welcome   1

Part 1 Preparing to Race   4

Race # 1 – What's Your Story   13

Race # 2 – Masks and Make-up   21

Race # 3 – Shaped, Not Defined   30

Race # 4 – Grieving Loss and Celebrating Love   39

Race # 5 – Looking for Love   49

Part 2 Halfway Mark   59

Race # 6 – Your Heart for Others   61

Race # 7 – Choosing Life and Health over Addiction   69

Race # 8 – Believing is Seeing   78

Race # 9 – Your Purpose and Dreams   87

Race # 10 – Finding Adventure   96

Appendix I – The Change Course Assessment   107

Conclusion: The Road Ahead   124

Leader Guide   125

Acknowledgments   129

Outline of Each Chapter:

This workbook is designed to be used in conjunction with my book, *Change Course: One Lady's Race from Acceptance to Adventure*. Each chapter of that book has a corresponding chapter (Race) in this workbook with various tools to help you see your story and change course to create your new life. Each race contains the following components:

- A brief synopsis of my story from the corresponding chapter of my book.

- "5-RACE" exercises to keep you on track and propel you forward.

- "Beyond the Finish Line"– some tips on digging deeper into the topic.

- A short prayer that you can use to connect your race with God.

Disclaimer:

This workbook comes from my personal experiences with changing course in my life. It is not intended to be taken as professional help. The nature of my story and the exercises contained in this workbook deal with healing your heart, mind and body. As you go through the exercises, you may identify that you need professional help to process what you are experiencing. Others are willing and able to help. Reach out and take their hand when you feel the need.

Welcome

Welcome to the companion workbook to *Change Course,* where you can track your ideas, thoughts, and progress. I found that I needed to write to heal myself. Early on, I felt my life story was more than just about me—it became about others too. I realized we are all connected through our stories because everyone has one. I wanted my story to help other people find the healing, love, acceptance, freedom, and adventure I found.

My hope is this workbook will give you inspiration to make your heart's spark come to life. Please come along for the ride and let me help you as I offer my hand. I've traveled down these roads before and can show you the potholes, twists, and turns you may see along the way. You have a lot to offer this world. We need you!"

As we link arms, we are better, stronger, and will overcome. One of my hobbies that I love is race car driving. It's a challenge and an adventure. It's why I titled my book *Change Course,* and it's why you'll see racing analogies and racing language throughout this workbook. I picture myself on your Pit Crew helping you get ready for the race. Then I'll shift gears and take on the role as the Pace Car driver, helping all the racers warm up for the race and keeping them safe when there is a condition issue on the track by guiding them to a slower speed until the danger has passed. Without Pit Crews and a Pace Car, the racers might not make it to the finish line. They could even crash and burn.

Sometimes, we feel like we will never see the checkered flag because there's too much of our "junk" on the track of life—things that we *haven't dealt with in healthy ways.* That was the case for me. Maybe it's something you're facing as well. If I didn't deal with my junk, I wouldn't have been able to publish my first book and this companion workbook.

Reclaim Control of Your Life Workbook

Research shows 80% of our thoughts can be negative.[1] Debris and junk in our mind and on our path keep making us go off course, taking the wrong path, even putting us in the ditch sometimes and can be challenging. That's okay, you can *Change Course* and get back on the road to success with intentional focus and practice. Reclaim control of your life and all that you have to offer. Dig deep within yourself, grab hold of your potential and believe you too can have a life worth living.

Do you need a nudge to start your engines? Throughout this workbook, I'll help you get warmed up for your race, your journey. I'll help you slow down and stay safe when you need to take some time to "clear the track." Embrace control of your best version and show the world your true, glorious self.

My faith and God's power transformed my heart and life. God healed me physically, spiritually, and emotionally, but I had to be a willing participant and not think I could do it alone. That's why I love these bible verses written by King David in the book of Psalms:

> *"Create in me a pure heart, O God,*
> *and renew a steadfast spirit within me…Restore to me the joy of your salvation*
> *and grant me a willing spirit, to sustain me."* (Psalm 51:10, 12 NIV)

I keep asking God to renew my spirit today and every day. I'm far from perfect, and I haven't fully arrived, but I always want to remain a willing participant—being willing to change course is the first step to seeing your heart's desire. Will you, with me, be willing to change course? That's where it all begins, *starting right where you are*. That's the starting line for the race you are about to embark on. I will be along for the ride as part of your Pit Crew and Pace Car, so know you are not alone.

My hope for you when you get to the finish line of this workbook is that your heart and mind are transformed and filled with love, joy, and peace. Not transformed because you read my story, but because you allowed yourself to imagine your victory with the help of God and others. Once you've been able to clear some of the junk and debris off the track of your life, you'll start dreaming again, reclaiming control, discovering your purpose for being here on this little

---

[1] Maria Millett, *Challenge Your Negative Thoughts.* Michigan State University Extension, (March 31, 2017)

Welcome

globe. As you create and discover, you may revive a dormant dream or restart a long-lost goal you had for your life. You'll now be in a place where you can put the pedal to the metal and move forward into your new life—you'll be headed to a life you will love. *Friends, start your engines and let's win this race together!*

Part 1: Preparing to Race

Some things in life require preparation before you dive into doing them—and racing is one of those. This journey you have decided to embark on to change course in your life, is also one you will need to plan for. Don't worry, I'll guide you to get prepared to race, and then guide you to the finish line.

Let's get started on your plan preparation. First, here is my R.A.C.E. strategy that helped me and may help you too. When I speak to groups about how I changed course in my life and how they can too, I use my R.A.C.E. acronym:

- R – Roadmap
- A – Acceptance
- C – Courage
- E – Energy

"R" is for Roadmap.

A roadmap is designed to help you stay true to who you are as you go from point A to point B. If you want to reach a different destination than where you are today, you'll need a map. For me, my faith is central to my life, therefore the Bible is part of my Roadmap. It guides me each step of the way until I get to my destination. Planning and preparation, with faith, and also with a Pit Crew, is how I start each race. As you embark on your own race to change course, you'll need your own roadmaps to point you in the right direction and keep you true to your values. This workbook can be one of the roadmaps to help get you to where you want to be. If you take a wrong turn, no worries—make adjustments, change course, and get back on track.

Part 1: Preparing to Race

"A" is for Acceptance.

Acceptance of self. You don't need this to begin your race, but you will need it to get to the finish line. This workbook will help you acquire self-acceptance along the way. For me, my self-acceptance is anchored in God's love for me. He loves me and He loves you too. In fact, He knows everything about you, loves you like crazy anyway, and He wants an intimate, loving relationship with YOU.

"C" is for Courage.

Courage is not the absence of fear, it's facing your fears and moving forward in spite of them; courage is faith over fear. I faced fears and obstacles on my journey to change course in my life and still do. Pressing into my fears with an ounce of grit and a pound of faith has resulted in getting me to a life I love. It can help you get there too.

"E" is for Energy.

By energy, I mean soul, heart, mind, body vitality, and physical health. I can't win a race if my car is out of fuel, has a flat tire, or there are bits of metal in my oil. I had to make changes in how I took care of myself in order to make other changes in my life. I couldn't do this race without nourishing my heart and soul with God's word, eating wholesome food, exercising and movement, getting rest, practicing meditation and general self-care. The same can be true for you. If you are worn down, worn out, sick, or out of fuel, you won't have the emotional and mental energy you'll need for the journey ahead.

Change Course Assessment

Every race has a starting point, and this is yours for this part of your life. Maybe you have already made a few laps around the track when it comes to healing and change. Maybe you are just beginning on this journey. To reach the destination you have in mind, you have to know where you are now. The *Change Course* Assessment found in Appendix 1. I will help you determine a starting point in your race. Turn there now to complete the assessment and see your results. Then, come back to this section to complete the next steps in preparation for your first race.

Next Steps After Assessment

Now that you know your starting point after taking the assessment, let's finish your race preparation with the five race exercises. Each one will prepare you to set the stage for your victory. They will become your strength and comfort as you use them for each race. You will become familiar with your track and gain the needed confidence to change course.

1. "S.H.I.F.T. Gears" – A Mindset Reset to Embrace Healing and Change

Do you ever have "stinking thinking"? You're not alone. Even the most positive people struggle with negative thoughts sometimes (me included). Our thoughts are incredibly powerful. They can propel us forward with confidence or cripple us with analysis paralysis. "S.H.I.F.T. Gears" is a mindset reset exercise that will help you take your thoughts captive—instead of them keeping you prisoner and holding you back from changing the course of your life.

S – Start Small
One thing that can stop change in its tracks is *the fear of failure.* Maybe you feel like all you do is fail, and you're afraid to go forward with this workbook because you think you'll fail again. Sometimes you need to experience a successful moment to adjust your mindset. *Start small* by setting mini goals that don't feel like they are too big to accomplish. Once you see what success feels like, you will want more of it.

List one small goal you can set today and achieve within the next week. (Example: Instead of trying to exercise every day, set a goal to do 5 pushups or walk in your neighborhood twice this week.)

H – Hang Up on the Past
When the past comes calling to remind you of all the times you have tried and failed

Part 1: Preparing to Race

before, hang up on it! How will you shut down the past before it ever gets started? Tell it to take a hike. It may sound silly at first, but by verbally "hanging up" on the past, you can continue pushing forward into the future.

Write out what you will say when the past comes calling. (Example: Past, I have blocked your number!)

I – Identify your Negative Thoughts

Did you know that you have automatic *negative thoughts* that have been programmed into your thinking since you were a child? Becoming aware of and identifying our *Negative Talk* will help us reset our mindset. List one *Negative Talk* that replays in your mind even though it is not welcomed. (Example: "I have always struggled with math," or "I have a big mouth just like my Aunt.")

F – Flip the Script

Negative Talk is important to recognize, and even more important to replace it with something positive. "Flip the Script means you turn any negative thoughts into positive thoughts by replacing them with a positive statement.

Write your "script flip" to the *Negative Talk* you listed above.

T – Take a Walk

Changing our physical position can create a physical change in our brains that allows us to change our thinking. If you need a mindset reset, go for a walk. Even moving in place with your eyes closed while visualizing a field of flowers or walking into another room can help our brain reset from what we were thinking a minute earlier. Don't believe me? When was the last time you walked into a room, but forgot why? "Take a walk" the next time you need a mindset reset. Record your experience here:

You did it. You have completed the first exercise to help prepare you for your race. Let's move on to the next step.

2. Build Your Pit Crew – Identifying a Team to Support Your Racing Efforts

A top Pit Crew is a "must have" for any successful race car driver. The crew is there to give a team's driver the best chance of winning the race. No racer wins by themselves; it is a team effort. The same is true for you. If you are going to reach the finish line when you change course in your life, you will need a team to "have your back" along the way.

Every member of the Pit Crew serves a different purpose. Some members change tires, some repair engine issues, others coach the driver. As you assemble your Pit Crew, look for people in your life who can serve different purposes. You will need some people who:

- Encourage you.

- Motivate and listen to you.

- Help you, especially during times of stress or disappointment.

Your Pit Crew can be made up of family, friends, life coach, pastor, mentor, or anyone you know who has your best interest at heart. As you recruit these people, tell them what you are up to and why you need their help. Let them know ahead of time what you specifically need from them in order to help you change course. In our race analogy, when your car (think body or mind) is broken down, you need a crew to rush in for the repairs.

List two to three people you can enlist to be in your Pit Crew.

3. Develop a Racing Strategy– Handling Potential Dangers and Setbacks

There is always a chance that something will go wrong in a race. The track has the potential to be slippery and dangerous. When I'm racing, it is impossible to predict if I am going to get a flat tire, hit a pothole, or need to dodge a crash ahead of me. However, I can be prepared with a strategy for what I will do when something unexpected comes up.

Part 1: Preparing to Race

Developing a "Racing Strategy" mindset will help you plan for the unexpected. Think of the potential issues you might encounter on your race to change course in your life. Decide ahead of time what you will do when your forward progress is halted.

- Do you have a plan for when a family member might want to derail your personal progress in telling your story, healing, and reclaiming your life's control?

- Do you tend to self-sabotage your progress prior to a breakthrough?

- Does the enemy/evil one/Satan try to distract or discourage you every time you dig deeper with God for His love, forgiveness, and guidance?

These questions will help you develop your strategy:

√ Who in my life may not be happy or supportive when I start making positive changes?

√ What boundaries will I put in place with this person, so he/she doesn't get me off-track?

√ What self-sabotaging behaviors do I sometimes exhibit when I am afraid of succeeding at something?

- √ How will I recognize when I am doing these things, and how will I stop?

- √ What will I do when I am distracted or discouraged from deepening my faith in God?

- √ What will I do the next time the enemy tries these tactics?

4. Celebrate the Victories– Tracking Progress and Enjoying the Journey

There is a difference between commuting to work and taking a road trip. Both involve driving, but one focuses on the destination while the other is about enjoying the journey. As you go through this race to change course in your life, it is important to remember that enjoying the journey is as important as reaching the destination. One way to do this is to celebrate the victories.

I started racing cars because it was always something I wanted to do. Of course, I wanted to win first place, but when I started racing, I didn't win first place right away. To keep going forward, I set milestones for progress and celebrated the small victories. I celebrated when I didn't come in last. I celebrated when I passed another racer on the track. I celebrated when I didn't get a flat tire. Every celebration of small victories led me to bigger victories and helped me enjoy the journey.

Part 1: Preparing to Race

**Set the big goals for your race to change course in your life.
Then set incremental milestones to ensure you enjoy
the journey and celebrate the victories.**

√ What does your life look like at the finish line?

√ What is the big change you want to make in your life? (Example: I want to break a bad habit, or I want to lose 30 lbs.)

√ Divide that goal into several small goals that become milestones in your journey to change course. (Example: Eliminate "fast food" from my diet.)

√ When you reach your milestone(s), how will you celebrate the victories? (Example: When I eat healthy food/fuel for one month, I'll get a massage.)

5. Start with a Spark – Discovering the "Why" Behind Your Race to Change Course

I mentioned before that when I started writing my book, the purpose was to tell my story, but then it became about helping others find love, acceptance, freedom, and adventure. My "why" behind writing my book became bigger than just a goal for me; it became a goal to inspire positive change in others. My "why" motivated me to keep moving toward the finish line. What started with a spark became the fuel for my journey ahead.

In the previous exercise, you described the change you want to see in your life. In this exercise, you will start to uncover your "why" behind it. Your "why" is what will keep you motivated as you change course in your life. Your "why" will help you finish your race, even when you feel like quitting.

- √ Why do you want to see the change in your life you described in the "Celebrate Victories" exercise? This is critical in the success of your journey; take time in determining your "why."

You did it! You've completed all the necessary preparation to begin racing towards your new life. Strap yourself in and start your engines!

Race #1: What's Your Story?

*"Everyone will share the story of your wonderful goodness;
they will sing with joy about your righteousness."*
(Psalm 145:7 NLT)

In Chapter 1 of *Change Course*, I reveal my experience about the first telling of my story. It was nerve-racking to put myself out there, but in the end, it gave me healing power—and became the catalyst for writing my book. The first telling of your story will be nerve-racking too. It's hard to be open and vulnerable. But when it is done in a safe environment, it is very liberating and healing.

In this chapter of the workbook, you will begin the process of telling your story. The great thing about storytelling is that you don't have to tell your entire story. You can pick a part of your story to tell. Maybe later you will want to tell a different part of your story. You own your story, and you decide when and to whom you want to share it with.

RECLAIM CONTROL OF YOUR LIFE WORKBOOK

Think of a time in your life when something happened that had a profound impact on you. It can be a big or small event. It can be something that meant a lot to you. List three to five events in your life that impacted you.

1.

2.

3.

4.

5.

Pick one of the above events and write a few sentences about it.

Do you see God in your story? If so, where?

Race 1: What's Your Story?

Now that you wrote part of your story, you get to tell it to someone. Look at your Pit Crew list you created in the "Preparing to Race" section. Which person on your list is the best listener? Who do you trust with your story? Arrange to call or meet with that person so you can tell the story you just wrote.

Race #1: Five Exercises

1. "S.H.I.F.T. Gears"

S = Start Small

How did you feel after accomplishing the task of telling just a small part of your story?

How do you think this small step could help you set and achieve other small goals?

H = Hang Up on the Past

Did your past disappointments come calling when you attempted to write and tell your story?

Race 1: What's Your Story?

Did you do something to "hang up on the past?"

I = Identify your Negative Talk

Did you notice any *Negative Talk* that came up as you were preparing to write or tell your story? If so, what were those thoughts?

F = Flip the Script

"Flip the Script" on the *Negative Talk* and turn each into a positive.

T = Take a Walk

At any time during the writing (or telling) of your story, did you "Take a walk" to change your thinking? If so, how did it help?

2. Building Your Pit Crew

Who did you choose, and how was the experience of telling your story to a trusted member of your Pit Crew?

How did telling your story change you or make you feel?

3. Developing a Race Strategy

Were there any dangers, resistance, or obstacles that came up as you were writing or telling your story? If so, what were they?

Race 1: What's Your Story?

What strategy will you implement to make sure those things don't trip you up in the future?

4. Celebrate the Victories

It's a huge victory to complete telling part of your story. How will you celebrate your achievement in this milestone moment?

5. Start with a Spark

How did explaining "WHY" you want to change course make you feel?

How did your trusted crew member react when you shared this with them?

Beyond the Finish Line:

Now that you have experienced writing and telling part of your story, keep going! Tell another part of your story, and then another, and maybe even another. You never know, you might end up with a blog, book or a podcast!

When we tell our story, we help others tell theirs. Who can you help encourage the first telling of their story? Write down that person's name and reach out to them. Who knows? You might be the catalyst for someone to start their own race.

The God Story:

Every part of our story is lovingly crafted by God. Your story is history—His story too. Let's take a minute to thank Him for it.

Dear God,
Thank you for the story you wrote for me. I may not like every part of it, but you have a purpose in every plot, character, and storyline. I thank you that my story is not over yet,
and You have more to write for me.
I trust that your love and grace will provide the perfect ending.
Amen.

Race #2: Masks and Makeup

"You made all the delicate, inner parts of my body and knit me together in my mother's womb. Thank you for making me so wonderfully complex! Your workmanship is marvelous—how well I know it."
(Psalm 139:13-14 NLT)

In Chapter 2 of *Change Course*, I share the story of my rare skin disease that left me with spots all over my body. Parents pointed and stared; and steered playmates away from me at the swimming pool. I wrote a coping song, *"Please don't hurt my little girl,"* and would sing it to myself. Later, I used makeup, long sleeves, and long pants to hide my spots.

Perhaps you have scars you are hiding from. Sometimes we hide behind makeup, sometimes it's a mask, pretending to be someone we're not. These behaviors can all have roots from the same issue: a lack of self-esteem and self-acceptance. And that usually stems from the lies we believe about ourselves.

It took me a long time to get to the point of self-acceptance and rebuild my self-esteem from the damage caused by others. I did it, and you can too! A big part of getting to that point has been embracing God's love for me, knowing He made me uniquely perfect, because I'm His beloved wonderfully made child. This is the truth I remind myself of in order to combat the lies. You too need to know that you are unique for a reason and loved unconditionally by God and others.

In this part of the workbook, you will go through an exercise in self-image. By the end of this exercise, I hope you are one step closer to seeing yourself as the beautiful creation you are!

Make a list of 10 characteristics about yourself that can be internal or external; positive or negative. Some positive traits to embrace and build on may include these examples: Compassion, Patience, Courage, Loyalty, Adaptability, Honesty, Responsible.

Here are some examples of negative traits a person can work on improving: Unforgiving, Passive-Aggressive, Judgmental, Vindictive, Manipulative, Dishonest, Lazy.
Your list will be unique to you.

Positive Traits	Negative Traits
1	1
2	2
3	3
4	4
5	5
6	6
7	7
8	8
9	9
10	10

Race 2: Masks and Makeup

For each one, write down the source of that message about yourself.

Next to each one, write: TRUTH or LIE.

Which have you written the most: TRUTH or LIE?

What do you have more of; positive attributes or negative attributes?

Go back to any attributes you labeled "LIE." How have these lies impacted the way you look at yourself?

What things have you tried to hide so no one would see them?

Has hiding helped or hurt your self-esteem?

Go back to any attributes you labeled "TRUTH." How have these truths impacted the way you look at yourself?

The Bible verse at the beginning of this chapter says that God "knit" or crafted every part of you, hidden and seen, and that He made you "wonderfully complex." When you think about God creating you uniquely and just like He designed you because He loves you, how does that impact the way you look at yourself?

Race 2: Masks and Makeup

Race #2: Five Exercises

1. "S.H.I.F.T. Gears"

S = Start Small
Set a small goal to say something **positive** about how God made you, or compliment yourself on something small you did or said each day for a week. Either of these small steps will help to reframe your view of yourself, improve your self-esteem, and lead you toward self-acceptance. Write out below what you said to yourself:

Sunday –

Monday –

Tuesday –

Wednesday –

Thursday –

Friday –

Saturday –

H = Hang Up on the Past

IF you wrote out negative instead of positive attributes, circle the "LIEs" and write what you say to the past about the LIE attributes when they come calling again.

Race 2: Masks and Makeup

I = Identify your Negative Talk

Did you notice any *Negative Talk* that came up as you were going through this exercise? If so, how did it make you feel?

F = Flip the Script

"Flip the Script" on each *Negative Talk* and turn it into a positive.

T = Take a Walk

At any time during this exercise, did you feel the desire to get up and "Take a walk?" That may have been your brain trying to help you change your thinking. Next time you feel the urge, take the walk.

2. Building Your Pit Crew

Select a member of your Pit Crew who knows you well. Tell the person about the exercises you completed for this chapter and ask them to give you a few positive attributes about yourself that you can add to your list. Write them below.

How does hearing someone else compliment you make you feel?

3. Developing a Race Strategy

Were there any dangers, resistance, or obstacles that came up as you were completing the exercise? If so, what were they?

What strategy will you implement to make sure those things don't trip you up in the future?

Race 2: Masks and Makeup

4. Celebrate the Victories

Working towards self-acceptance is a big victory. How will you celebrate your achievement in this milestone moment?

5. Start with a Spark

How does changing the way you think about yourself fit into your "why" behind the course change that you want to make in your life?

Beyond the Finish Line:

Improving your self-esteem and getting to self-acceptance is a long race. You will need to continue to retrain your brain on what an amazing job God did when He made you. Don't give up! Keep coming back to this exercise whenever your self-esteem crashes and you find yourself hiding behind masks or makeup.

God Broke the Mold:

God broke the mold when He made you, literally. There is not another you! Take a moment to thank God for how He created you.

Dear God,
Thank you for crafting me together the way you did. You broke the mold when you made me and created each aspect of me with love and purpose.
Please help me to see how wonderfully and beautifully complex I am.
Amen

Race #3: Shaped, Not Defined

"Our past may shape us, but it doesn't define who we become."
(Alyson Noel)

In Chapter 3 of *Change Course*, I talk about my childhood and the changes that occurred in my family. My parents divorced when my father left my mother for another woman. Then my mother married the ex-husband of my father's new wife. I called it the Parent Swap. These events shaped me in many ways, but so did other things. I had an absent father, but a very present and loving grandfather. Through the marriage, I gained several siblings who were previously my friends. My mom and stepdad fostered many children when our home became an emergency shelter home.

Some of my early family experiences shaped me negatively, and some shaped me positively—but they all shaped me. Yes, they shaped me, but they didn't define me. There is a difference. Understanding that difference will help with your race to change course.

Race 3: Shaped, Not Defined

Every part of our lives is woven together by a loving God. Nothing that happens to us is a surprise to Him. He can use every bit and piece of our functional and dysfunctional family for good in our lives. It may not always look good when it happens, but hindsight can be a good teacher.

In this chapter, you will go through an exercise that will highlight *defining moments or milestones in your early life*. My hope is that on the other side of this exercise, you too will be able to see the good that was shaped in you through these events, and how God is still using them today to show you His love for you.

In each of the following segments of your life, write down defining moments, major milestones, or relational changes and influences from your early life. No need to get specific, just provide a statement or phrase that describes the events or changes.

- Birth to Age Five

- Elementary School

- Middle School/Junior High

- High School

- Early 20s

Look back at your list of milestones and underline each event that had a negative impact on you. Then circle each event that had a positive impact on you.

Pick one of the milestones of your life and describe how it has shaped you.

Pick one of the milestones of your life and describe how you have allowed it to define you.

Race 3: Shaped, Not Defined

Flip the script of the milestone you had allowed to define you by reflecting on it *as a shaping event—instead of a defining event.*

Where do you see God in the events you recorded?

Was there any time when you sensed God was more present or less present in your life?

Race #3: Five Exercises

1. "S.H.I.F.T. Gears"

S = Start Small

Set a small goal to keep chipping away at the rest of the milestones on your listing, re-framing the narrative in a positive way for those that you have allowed to define you negatively. Pick one per week and journal the changes below.

H = Hang Up on the Past

Going through this exercise is certain to make the past come calling—that's the point. However, you won't want the past to keep calling after you have put it into the proper perspective. Limit the call time that the past gets, so you don't get stuck in a lengthy conversation with it.

Race 3: Shaped, Not Defined

I = Identify your Negative Talk

Did you notice any *Negative Talk* that came up as you were going through this exercise? If so, what were they?

F = Flip the Script

"Flip the Script" on the *Negative Talk* and turn them into a positive.

T = Take a Walk

As you go through expanding this exercise, try to "Take a walk" each time you need to change your thinking and rewrite the narrative. Even a walk to another room can help!

2. Building Your Pit Crew

Select a member of your Pit Crew who is familiar with some of the milestones of your past. Tell them about the exercise you completed for this chapter and share with them one that has defined you, and how you are rewriting the narrative to have it be only a positive-shaping experience.

How did it feel to tell someone else about your shift in thinking on this milestone?

3. Developing a Race Strategy

Were there any dangers, resistance, or obstacles that came up as you were completing the exercise? If so, what were they?

Race 3: Shaped, Not Defined

What strategy will you implement to make sure those things don't trip you up in the future?

4. Celebrate the Victories

Facing life's formative events is a big victory. How will you celebrate your achievement in this moment?

5. Start with a Spark

Did this exercise help you think differently about your "why" behind the course change you want to make in your life? Why or why not?

Beyond the Finish Line:

Looking back at past events of our childhood can be heavy work. This isn't a "one-and-done" type of exercise. As you race to change course, and keep pressing towards the life you want, you'll need to go back to each of those milestones and process through the questions and reflection exercises in this chapter. If you don't do the hard and heavy work on this, those milestones can turn into millstones that weigh you down, turning them into hazards on the track in your new life. Celebrate where you have been and what you learned from those experiences as they propel you into your future victory.

God's Timeline:

Nothing in your milestone timeline was a surprise to God. Every part of your life was lovingly woven by Him. Take a few minutes to thank Him for your life events.

Dear God,
Thank you for my life and the ways it has shaped me into the person I am today. There are some parts of it that I don't understand, and others that blow me away. I see your hand in my life story and am thankful that you have been with me every step of the way, even when I didn't see you. I'm thankful that you can use even the bad things for good. I'm excited to see the events you have lovingly planned for me in the future.
Amen.

Race #4: Grieving Loss and Celebrating Love

"The LORD gave, and the LORD has taken away; blessed be the name of the LORD."
(Job 1:21b ESV)

In Chapter 4 of *Change Course*, I share the painful life event of my brother Scott dying unexpectedly in a car accident. His death changed our lives forever, and his memory is still alive within us today. Other kinds of losses happen in our lives other than the death of a loved one who is precious to us. Shortly after my brother died, we moved to Ohio and I no longer was able to see my dear grandpa with whom I was very close. Despite all that loss in a short period of time, I was still able to celebrate the love I shared with all of them.

During my divorces and years later, I struggled with the loss of those relationships. Annoying negative chatter was replayed in my mind, and it needed to be shut down. Eventually I was able to forgive my ex-husbands—as well as myself for the part I played in the divorces—and to accept God's love and forgiveness.

Reclaim Control of Your Life Workbook

In this chapter of the workbook, you will identify areas of loss in your life and learn a few ways to grieve those losses. You will also identify key relationships in your life and learn how to celebrate them.

Grieving Loss

Which of the following losses have you experienced over your life so far? Circle all that apply.

Death of a parent	Loss of a job
Death of a spouse	Loss of a friendship
Death of a child	Divorce
Death of a friend	Bankruptcy
Death of a sibling	Foreclosure
Death of another loved one	Moving to a new place
Chronic disease or illness	Other:
Financial loss	

Of all the losses you circled, which one has been the hardest to process your grief?

Of the losses you circled, are there any you hadn't really considered a loss to grieve *until now*? Why or why not?

Take one of the losses you circled or wrote in and answer the following questions:

Race 4: Grieving Loss and Celebrating Love

1. What did I lose when this loss occurred? (This may sound obvious, but there are usually multiple losses wrapped up in a loss.)

2. Which of the losses listed do you miss the most and why?

3. What would my life look like today if that loss hadn't occurred?

4. What is better in my life now because that loss occurred? (Looking for the positive in a hard situation can be hard, so have grace with yourself and the situation.)

These four difficult questions can reveal a lot about how you have processed or are still processing loss, and how you persevered. As you look at your answers to the four questions, what stands out to you that you never noticed before?

Celebrating and Honoring Love

List below at least three names and roles of every key loving relationship in your life, whether they are still in your life today or not.

Circle three names that you would like to celebrate and honor.

For each of the three names, answer the following questions.

1. Why do I consider this person a key relationship in my life?

Race 4: Grieving Loss and Celebrating Love

2. How has this person helped make my life better?

3. How have I helped make this person's life better?

4. How can I celebrate and honor this person to show gratitude for their love?

Race #4: Five Exercises

1. "S.H.I.F.T. Gears"

S = Start Small

Set a goal to follow through with celebrating *one* of the people from the "Celebrate and Honoring Love" exercise. You can choose to do more later.

H = Hang Up on the Past

The past is going to haunt your mind when you go through the Grieving Loss exercise in this chapter—and it may remind you of all you have lost and how unfair life can be. Write what you learned or gained through your loss experiences.

Race 4: Grieving Loss and Celebrating Love

I = Identify your Negative Talk

Did you notice any *Negative Talk* that came up as you were going through this exercise? If so, what were these points?

F = Flip the Script

"Flip the Script" on the *Negative Talk* and turn them into a positive.

T = Take a Walk

As you went through this exercise, how many times did you "Take a walk?" If you did, how did it help? If you didn't, how could it have helped?

Reclaim Control of Your Life Workbook

2. Building Your Pit Crew

Select a member of your Pit Crew who knows about one of your losses. Tell them about the exercise you completed for this chapter and share one thing that stood out.

How did it help you to talk to someone about your loss?

3. Developing a Race Strategy

Were there any dangers, resistance, or obstacles that came up as you were completing the exercise? If so, what were they?

What strategy will you implement to make sure those things don't trip you up in the future?

Race 4: Grieving Loss and Celebrating Love

4. Celebrate the Victories

Exploring your loss and love *are huge victories.* Congrats! How will you celebrate your achievement in this moment?

5. Start with a Spark

Did looking at loss and love change your "why" behind the course change you want to make in your life? Why or why not?

Beyond the Finish Line:

If you need to do some more exploring of your losses and loves so you can change course and live the life you want, then go back and complete the questions for all your losses (or even just one more). Or you can go back and pick a few more key loving relationships to celebrate and honor.

God's Gifts:

In the Bible, a man named Job lost everything, I mean EVERYTHING! After he lost all 10 of his children in one day, he said the words quoted at the beginning of this chapter: *"The LORD gave, and the LORD has taken away; blessed be the name of the LORD."* In essence, Job thanked God for both the giving and the taking away. Both loss and love can be gifts from God if we choose to receive them as such. Take a minute to thank God for both.

Dear God,
Thank you for the gift of people in my life who I love and who love me. I am richly blessed!
And thank you for all those things you saw fit to take away. The losses are painful.
Please help me to learn from my losses and not cling to them.
Help me to celebrate those I love every day.
Amen.

Race #5: Looking for Love

*"But God showed his great love for us by sending
Christ to die for us while we were still sinners."*
(Romans 5:8 NLT)

In Chapter 5 of *Change Course*, I shared the stories of my marriages and divorces (yes, multiple). This was a hard chapter to write because all my failures were on pages for everyone to see. It was important for me to be real so other people can find healing and love after their own "mistakes."

As I mentioned in my story, I was haunted by my sin and mistakes for many years. I spent a long time looking for love and acceptance from the wrong kinds of men—and found it hard to feel worthy of love, especially God's love. In my healing journey, I came to find out that God loved me in my sin and loved me through my mistakes. Accepting God's unconditional love allowed me to find love with my husband Jim. (We celebrated 16 years of marriage in 2020). Maybe you've made some mistakes in relationships and have been haunted by your own past sins and feel unloved by God. Don't worry, if there was hope for me, there's hope for you too.

Reclaim Control of Your Life Workbook

In this chapter of the workbook, you'll identify crucial relationships in your life, look for behavior patterns, and notice where you might be looking for love and acceptance.

Make a list of all the crucial relationships in your life. This can include a father, mother, brother, sister, boyfriend, girlfriend, friend, mentor, spouse, or others. These are men/women who loved you or you loved them. (You can also add current people into this exercise.)

Go back to your list and underline all the negative relationships. (Those who mistreated you, abused you, or didn't value you or your contributions to the relationship. Or maybe you are in a current negative relationship and need to recognize those as well.)

How did/does this person make you feel about yourself?

When you look at the names of the people you underlined, what were you hoping to receive from them in return for your love?

Race 5: Looking for Love

Why didn't you receive what you were hoping for?

Did you make poor decisions or mistakes when you didn't receive what you were looking for?

What were they?

Now go back to your list and circle all the names of people who impacted you positively. (Those who made you feel safe and loved. Those who valued, loved and respected you.) How did these people make you feel about yourself?

When you look at the names you circled, what was it that you received from them?

Were there good or wise decisions you made because of how they loved and cared for you?

What were they?

Did you make relationship mistakes that you are still feeling guilty about? Why or why not?

Race 5: Looking for Love

If you knew *God loved you unconditionally*, would that change the type of people you choose to have key relationships with? Why or why not?

What steps can you take to discover and accept God's forgiveness and love for you?

Race #5: Five Exercises

1. "S.H.I.F.T. Gears"

S = Start Small

Set a goal to learn one new thing about God's love once a week for the next month. Look up bible verses or ask a friend. Write what you learn below:

Week 1:

Week 2:

Week 3:

Week 4:

Race 5: Looking for Love

H = Hang Up on the Past

I'm sure the past came to mind strongly during this exercise. When the past haunts you about relationship failures, what will you say to cut the call short?

I = Identify your Negative Talk

Did you notice any *Negative Talk* that came up as you were going through this exercise? If so, what were they?

F = Flip the Script

"Flip the Script" on the *Negative Talk* and turn them into a positive.

Reclaim Control of Your Life Workbook

T = Take a Walk

As you went through this exercise, how many times did you "Take a walk?" If you did, how did it help? If you didn't, how could it have helped?

2. Building Your Pit Crew

Select a member of your Pit Crew who knows about some of your crucial relationships. Tell them about the exercise you completed for this chapter and share with them one thing that stood out the most to you as you went through it. How did it help you to talk to someone about what you learned?

3. Developing a Race Strategy

Were there any dangers, resistance, or obstacles that came up as you were completing the exercise? If so, what were they?

Race 5: Looking for Love

What strategy will you implement to make sure those things don't trip you up in the future?

4. Celebrate the Victories

Making headway on your relationships is a victory worth celebrating. Congrats! How will you celebrate your achievement in this moment?

5. Start with a Spark

Does the life you want include better relationships? How does this exercise help you toward that? Did it change your "why" behind the course change you want to make in your life? Why or why not?

Beyond the Finish Line:

There are levels to explore in our relationships. If you want to go deeper, continue the exercise from this chapter with more of your crucial relationships, adding more details to your answers.

God's Love:

The fact that God loves us unconditionally is hard to accept, especially if none of our human relationships have that kind of love in them. It's also hard to accept if you are carrying the weight of unforgiveness on your back. Take a minute to talk to God about it.

Dear God,
I have a hard time believing you would love me after how I've been loved by others.
I don't understand your unconditional love, but I accept it.
Thank you for loving me in spite of myself and my mistakes. I am tired of carrying guilt and shame around. I bring it to you and ask you, God, to forgive me.
Thank you!
Amen.

Part 2: Halfway Mark

You did it! You've made it halfway through this workbook. The halfway mark is a great time to pause and look at the progress you've made—and to change course where needed.

Take a look at your findings from the assessment you took that's in Appendix I. On the line graphs located in your findings, mark where you are making progress by putting a star where you think you are today. Then answer the following questions:

Where do you see the most movement so far?

Why do you think you are making a lot of progress there?

Where do you see yourself stuck in neutral, or moving in reverse?

Why do you think that is happening? What do you need to do to move forward?

How will you celebrate your small and big victories?

Race #6: Your Heart for Others

"There's no way to be a perfect mother and a million ways to be a good one."
(Jill Churchill)

In Chapter 6 of *Change Course*, I reflect on motherhood as my favorite occupation. If it were any other occupation, I should have been fired a few times based on my poor performance. I did the best I could with what I had. Isn't that what all mother and fathers are trying to do? The best they can? Both my daughters and step-son are grown now, and I have been promoted to grand-motherhood! It seems like there is so much pressure for mothers to be perfect these days; the joy of motherhood sometimes gets lost in the chaos.

In this chapter, if you are a parent, you will go through an exercise to recount the joys of your parenting experience and release your regrets over any mistakes. If you are not a parent either by choice or circumstance, ask your mother or father the questions, if possible. You might learn something about your parent and yourself in the process. If your parents are not available to do this, write a note thanking them for being your parent, sharing one fond memory

ped in and filled the role as your
you have from your childhood. If you had someone that stepped in and filled the role as your parent, you can do this exercise with them. All families are unique, so adjust as needed.

Looking back on your early parenting days, for each of your children, list one of your biggest joys or a memorable moment that made you glad you were their parent.

For each of your children, write out your hopes and dreams for them today. (No matter how old they are!)

What is one thing you know now that you want to tell your younger self about parenting?

List one moment when you felt like you "blew it" as a parent.

Race 6: Your Heart for Others

Holding onto regrets can keep you from changing course to live the life you want. Write a note to yourself forgiving yourself for "blowing it," and releasing any regret you still feel.

If you could say anything encouraging to a mother or father of little ones today, what would it be?

Race #6: Five Exercises

1. "S.H.I.F.T. Gears"

S = Start Small

Set a goal to send each child a note about your biggest joy in parenting them. If it is not possible to share with your child, you can still write and share it with someone in your Pit Crew.

H = Hang Up on the Past

When the past came calling to tell you to hang onto your parenting regrets, what did you say to hang up on it?

Race 6: Your Heart for Others

I = Identify your Negative Talk

Did you notice any *Negative Talk* that came up as you were going through this exercise? If so, what were they?

F = Flip the Script

"Flip the Script" on the *Negative Talk* and turn them into a positive.

T = Take a Walk

As you went through this exercise, how many times did you "Take a walk?" If you did, how did it help? If you didn't, how could it have helped?

2. Building Your Pit Crew

Select a member of your Pit Crew who is a parent. Tell them about the exercise you completed for this chapter and share with them one thing that stood out the most to you as you went through it. How did it help you to talk to someone about what you learned?

3. Developing a Race Strategy

Were there any dangers, resistance, or obstacles that came up as you were completing the exercise? If so, what were they?

What strategy will you implement to make sure those things don't trip you up in the future?

Race 6: Your Heart for Others

4. Celebrate the Victories

Dealing with regrets is one way to find healing—and it deserves a celebration. Congrats! How will you celebrate your achievement in this moment?

5. Start with a Spark

Did this exercise affect your "why" behind the course change you want to make in your life? Why or why not?

Beyond the Finish Line:

If you want to go deeper in this exercise, take the same questions to your own mother, father, another family member, or Pit Crew person you know, and then go through it with them. This will help them remember joy and release the regrets.

God's Love for your Children:

Did you know that God talks about His love for us and sometimes compares it to a mother's love? God gives children to us as a gift, but they belonged to Him before they became ours. Take a minute to thank God for your children (and/or your mother) and release them to Him.

Dear God,
Thank you for giving me the gift of my children (and/or my mother). I can see your unconditional love for me in the way I unconditionally love my children/mother. I want only what's best for them—and what's best for them is you. I release my children/mother to you and ask you to make yourself and your love known to them.
Amen.

Race #7: Choosing Life and Health over Addiction

"The temptations in your life are no different from what others experience. And God is faithful. He will not allow the temptation to be more than you can stand. When you are tempted, he will show you a way out so that you can endure."
(1 Corinthians 10:13 NLT)

In *Change Course*, I shared about my husband's struggle with his addiction to alcohol. In Chapter 7, I shared my stepdad's struggles with his sugar addiction, as well as my own addiction to sugar. I explained my journey to good health, or energy as I like to call it—energy to live the life I want.

Addiction comes in many forms. We may be familiar with addiction to alcohol and/or drugs, but we often overlook addictions to sugar, salt, food, weight loss, compulsive exercise, shopping, gambling, pornography, social media, work, and unfortunately, the list goes on. In this chapter of the workbook, you will identify any addictive behaviors you may have and reflect on how you can get energy for the life you want to live.

What is one thing you consistently do when you are stressed out or anxious?

What do you consistently turn to when you want to numb feelings of pain, loss, or failure?

What behaviors do you engage in consistently when you are bored or lonely?

Do you or have you ever struggled in the past with an addiction to anything? If so, what is it?

Race 7: Choosing Life and Health over Addiction

How do/did you feel when you engaged in that addiction?

How do/did you feel when you couldn't engage in that addiction?

True or False: My addictive behavior is hindering me from living the life I want.

Are you willing to stop your addictive behavior and/or get professional help so you can change course?

　　___Yes (with the help of God and others).　　___ No, I am not ready.

What changes do you need to make to get the energy (health, vitality, faith), you need to change course and live the life you want? (List all that apply. They can be addressed in small steps later.)

Race 7: Choosing Life and Health over Addiction

Race #7: Five Exercises

1. "S.H.I.F.T. Gears"

S = Start Small

Set a goal to start making some changes to replace addiction with positive energy. You may choose to turn your phone off at 7 p.m. tonight or drink three additional glasses of water tomorrow. You decide what your one small step will be and then write it below.

Place a deadline on this step and add it to your calendar or planner.

H = Hang Up on the Past

Did the past come calling when you started thinking about making the changes needed to fight your addiction and then gain health? What did it say?

What did you say back?

What will you say back in the future?

I = Identify your Negative Talk

Did you notice any *Negative Talk* that came up as you were going through this exercise? If so, what were they?

Race 7: Choosing Life and Health over Addiction

F = Flip the Script

"Flip the Script" on the *Negative Talk* and turn them into a positive.

T = Take a Walk

As you went through this exercise, how many times did you "Take a walk?" If you did, how did it help? If you didn't, how could it have helped?

2. Building Your Pit Crew

Select a member of your Pit Crew you trust. Tell them about the exercise you completed for this chapter and share with them the one small step you are going to take to start making changes. Ask them to hold you accountable. How does it help to talk to someone about what you want to change?

3. Developing a Race Strategy

Were there any dangers, resistance, or obstacles that came up as you were completing the exercise? If so, what were they?

What strategy will you implement to make sure those things don't trip you up in the future?

4. Celebrate the Victories

Taking a step towards gaining control over your addictions and health is a big victory. Congrats! How will you celebrate your achievement in this moment?

Race 7: Choosing Life and Health over Addiction

5. Start with a Spark

Did this exercise affect your "why" behind the course change you want to make in your life? Why or why not?

Beyond the Finish Line:

If you are just starting this journey to change course on your addiction and health, take one day at a time. This is a lifelong journey for all of us and we need to be intentional for the rest of our lives. The prize is worth it! Don't stop at your small step. After you complete that one step, set another small step and another until all those small steps add up to a giant leap forward.

God's Help:

One thing my husband Jim taught me: when he wants to drink, he must turn it over to God. Take a minute to turn your addictions and health over to God. He's great at listening and helping us all.

Dear God,
I am struggling with my addiction to _____.
I need your help. I know I need to make some changes if I am going to change course and live the fullest life you have for me. Please help me to keep taking small steps, one at a time. Thank you for your grace and love.
Amen

Race #8: Believing is Seeing

"Call to me and I will answer you. I'll tell you marvelous and wondrous things that you could never figure out on your own."
(Jeremiah 33:3 MSG)

In Chapter 8 of *Change Course*, I share my faith journey with God. I share my childhood faith, spurred on by my mother; my years of being far from God; my time as a "convenient Christian"; and the deepening of my faith through the years. I also share my physical experiences with God's healing light, which occurred twice in my life. Because of the white light healings, I have been seeking God all the more and is the driving force behind wanting to love more and help others.

Maybe you can relate to some of my experiences, maybe you can't. That's the thing, God wants to have a relationship with everyone, and since He made us all unique, that relationship is going to be unique for you.

Race 8: Believing is Seeing

I don't know where you are at in your relationship with God, or your journey of faith, but this chapter of the workbook will give you a chance to explore that, even if it's something you haven't paid much attention to until now. Maybe you aren't ready to go down that road right now; then you need to come back to this chapter later. That's okay. Just remember, we are made of both physical and spiritual beings. The spiritual side of your life will add fullness and joy to that new life you want to live.

What are your earliest memories around God and faith?

Did you have anyone in your early life who encouraged you to seek God? Who was it, and how did they guide your faith?

Did you ever go through a period in your life when you felt far away from God? Describe that time in your life.

Reclaim Control of Your Life Workbook

Did you ever go through a period in your life when you felt especially close to God? Describe that time in your life.

If God was sitting next to you right now, what would you say to Him?

God is always speaking to us, but we aren't always listening. He speaks in multiple ways and one way is through His word, the Bible. Read the following verses from God's word and answer the questions for reflection below each one.

> *"For I know the plans I have for you," declares the LORD, "plans to prosper you and not to harm you, plans to give you hope and a future."*
> (Jeremiah 29:11 NIV)

What do you hear God saying to you personally as you read this declaration from Him?

Race 8: Believing is Seeing

*"Look! I stand at the door and knock. If you hear my voice and open the door,
I will come in, and we will share a meal together as friends."*
(Revelation 3:20 NLT)

What do you hear God saying to you personally as you read this invitation from Him?

"For the hearts of these people are hardened, and their ears cannot hear, and they have closed their eyes—so their eyes cannot see, and their ears cannot hear, and their hearts cannot understand, and they cannot turn to me and let me heal them."
(Matthew 13:15 NLT)

What do you hear God saying to you personally as He shares His heart?

Did you find this exercise easy or difficult, and why?

Race #8: Five Exercises

1. "S.H.I.F.T. Gears"

S = Start Small

Hearing God takes practice and quiet. Set a small goal to practice listening to God once a week. You can try a verse exercise like the one above, or just talk to Him like you would to a friend, and then listen to how He speaks to your heart. Schedule this weekly listening time on your calendar or planner.

H = Hang Up on the Past

Did the past come calling when you started thinking about God? What did it say?

What did you say back?

Race 8: Believing is Seeing

What will you say back in the future?

I = Identify your Negative Talk

Did you notice any *Negative Talk* that came up as you were going through this exercise?

If so, what were they?

F = Flip the Script

"Flip the Script" on the *Negative Talk* and turn them into a positive.

T = Take a Walk

As you went through this exercise, did you sense the need to "Take a walk?" If you did take a walk, how did it help? If you didn't, how could it have helped?

2. Building Your Pit Crew

Select a member of your Pit Crew who listens to God. Tell them about the exercise you completed for this chapter and share with them one thing that stood out to you in it. Ask them to share some of their experiences of listening to God. How did hearing another person's experiences with God help you reflect on your own?

3. Developing a Race Strategy

Were there any dangers, resistance, or obstacles that came up as you were completing the exercise? If so, what were they?

Race 8: Believing is Seeing

What strategy will you implement to make sure those things don't trip you up in the future?

4. Celebrate the Victories

Faith is a very personal thing to explore and share, but you did it! Congrats! How will you celebrate your achievement in this moment?

5. Start with a Spark

Did this exercise affect your "why" behind the course change you want to make in your life? Why or why not?

Beyond the Finish Line:

Wherever you are in your faith journey, there is always room to go deeper. As you begin your "start-small" exercise once a week, try to add in additional days to your goals. Being around other people on a faith journey helped my faith to grow. I encourage you to find a faith community and class about God or the Bible that you can take with other people. Most of all, get to know God and His heart for you.

God's Desire:

God desires to have a relationship with you, but you decide how deep it goes and if it grows. Seek Him and take a minute to talk to God about your desires in response to His desires. He is always ready and waiting with open arms.

Dear God,
When I think about the fact that you love me, I feel overwhelmed and unworthy, but I thank you for your love. Thank you for being with me throughout my life, even when I was distant and didn't want to spend time with you. I am thankful you want to have an intimate relationship with me. I want to have one with you too and get to know you better. I want to learn to listen when you speak and see you work in my life.
Amen.

Race #9: Your Purpose and Dreams

"All our dreams can come true, if we have the courage to pursue them."
(Walt Disney)

In Chapter 9 of *Change Course*, I share various dreams I've had and how some went the way I had hoped they would, but others didn't. I listed my career progression, my modeling dreams, and businesses that succeeded but then didn't go as planned. Each step along the way, I learned to keep dreaming, dust myself off, and get going again.

In this chapter of the workbook, you will get to revisit your dreams and let your spark for those new dreams and desires come to life.

What is something that you always wanted to do when you were younger?

If money were no object, what would you do with your time?

What needs or causes do you care most about?

What have you always been good at?

Who do you admire the most? And why?

Race 9: Your Purpose and Dreams

Think of a time when you felt fulfilled, satisfied, or most alive. What were you doing at that time?

Based on your answers above, list one to three dreams you would like to have or accomplish or experience in the new life you are creating as you change course.

1.

2.

3.

Race #9: Five Exercises

1. **"S.H.I.F.T. Gears"**

   ### S = Start Small

   Sometimes we don't accomplish our dreams and change course in our lives because it looks too big and scary to accomplish. *What is one small thing you can do this week to start moving towards your dreams and the new life you want?* Schedule it on your calendar or planner. (Example: Find someone who has already accomplished what you want to do and set up time to talk to them about how they did it. Research organizations that help the cause that interests you.)

   ### H = Hang Up on the Past

   Did the past come calling when you started thinking about dreams you've tried before, but failed at making the dream a reality? What did it say?

   What did you say back?

Race 9: Your Purpose and Dreams

What will you say back in the future?

I = Identify your Negative Talk

Did you notice any *Negative Talk* that came up as you were going through this exercise? If so, what were they?

F = Flip the Script

"Flip the Script" on the *Negative Talk* and turn them into a positive.

T = Take a Walk

As you went through this exercise, did you sense the need to "Take a walk?" If you did take a walk, how did it help? If you didn't, how could it have helped?

2. Building Your Pit Crew

Select a member of your Pit Crew who has accomplished one of their dreams. Tell them about the exercise you completed for this chapter and share with them one thing that stood out to you in it. Ask them to share some of their experiences in successfully chasing their dreams.

How did hearing another person's experiences help motivate you to pursue your own dreams?

Race 9: Your Purpose and Dreams

3. Developing a Race Strategy

What dangers, resistance, or obstacles could keep you from chasing your dreams and living the life you want?

What strategy will you implement to make sure those things don't stop you?

4. Celebrate the Victories

You came up with some new dreams. Congrats! How will you celebrate your achievement in this moment?

5. Start with a Spark

Did this exercise affect your "why" behind the course change you want to make in your life? Why or why not?

Beyond the Finish Line:

This is only the beginning of the new life you want. Keep breaking your dreams into small steps until you accomplish them. Don't give up! Don't let things distract you and/or allow other people to derail you. Keep going for what you want, even if it takes you outside your comfort zone. You will encounter hard work and struggles as you change course to transform your life, but it is worth it!

God's Dreams:

I believe God puts dreams (a.k.a. "spark") in our hearts because He wants us to accomplish the plans and purposes He has for our lives.

As we take steps towards our dreams, God guides and helps us along the way.

> *"Your word is a lamp to my feet and a light for my path."*
> (Psalm 116:105 NIV)

Race 9: Your Purpose and Dreams

Take a minute to tell God about your dreams and ask for His guidance.

Dear God,
I have a dream to _____.
This dream is both scary and exciting to me. I believe you put this dream/spark in my heart because you have only good plans and purposes for me. Please direct my steps and help me along the way so I can see your plans for me come to pass.
Amen.

Race #10: Finding Adventure

"...the joy of the Lord is your strength!"
(Nehemiah 8:10b NLT)

In Chapter 10 of *Change Course*, I share my passion and joy for racing—one of my dreams that came true for me. I also talk about the dreams of writing this book and my dreams to speak to others about what I've learned. None of these things were easy, but they were all adventures for me. I enjoy trying new things and stepping out in faith even when it's scary. If life was easy all the time, would it be satisfying and fulfilling? Trying new things is how we change course and create the life we want. Trying new things is how our dreams come true. And in that, we find joy in living a fulfilling life.

In this chapter of the workbook, you will identify adventures (a.k.a. new things), that you would like to try. They might be part of your dreams from the previous chapter, or they might be something completely different.

Race 10: Finding Adventure

The definition of an adventure is an exciting or unusual experience that usually involves some type of risks. Based on that definition, list five things you would consider to be an "adventure" that you would like to try. It can be taking a college class or going skydiving. It just has to be something that challenges you to move outside your comfort zone.

1.

2.

3.

4.

5.

Why do you want to try these things?

How do each of these move you outside your comfort zone?

Make a list of the steps you would need to take to experience the adventure that most excites you.

How would this adventure bring joy to your life?

Would this adventure increase your confidence to try other adventures? Why or why not?

Race #10: Five Exercises

1. "S.H.I.F.T. Gears"

S = Start Small

This week do the *first thing* on the list of steps you need to take to experience your adventure. Schedule the second step on your calendar or planner for next week.

H = Hang Up on the Past

Did the past come calling when you started thinking about moving outside your comfort zone? What did it say? What did you say back?

What will you say back in the future?

I = Identify your Negative Talk

Did you notice any *Negative Talk* that came up as you were going through this exercise? If so, what were they?

F = Flip the Script

"Flip the Script" on the *Negative Talk* and turn them into a positive.

T = Take a Walk

As you went through this exercise, did you "Take a walk?" If you did take a walk, how did it help? If you didn't, how could it have helped?

Race 10: Finding Adventure

2. Building Your Pit Crew

Select a member of your Pit Crew and tell them about the first adventure you want to try. Ask for their help in holding you accountable to take the steps needed to get there. Better yet, see if they want to join you! How did sharing your adventure dreams with someone motivate you to go for it?

3. Developing a Race Strategy

What dangers, resistance, or obstacles could keep you from your adventure?

What strategy will you implement to make sure those things don't stop you?

4. Celebrate the Victories

You are about to embark on your adventure. Congrats! How will you celebrate your achievement in this moment?

5. Start with a Spark

Does your adventure help fuel your "why" behind the course change you want to make in your life? Why or why not?

Beyond the Finish Line:

Once you complete your first adventure (congratulations!), write down your experience below.

Now select another one from your list and use the same process to go after it.

Race 10: Finding Adventure

God's Joy:

God wants to see us enjoy life to the fullest. Part of that includes taking risks and trying new things. Take a minute to tell God about the adventures you want to take. Ask Him to give you the courage to follow through with His help.

Dear God,
I want to go on an adventure where I _____.
Thank you for wanting to give me joy in this life.
Please help me to move outside my comfort zone and enjoy the ride!
Amen.

You did it!

You have completed the exercises to change course—and create the life you want! You've made a lot of progress and changes as you worked through this workbook. Let's measure that progress by revisiting your Change Course Assessment.

Review your assessment findings again in Appendix I. Mark with a star where you think you are today. Then answer the following questions:

Where do you see yourself moving in reverse?

Why do you think that is happening?

Where do you see yourself stuck in neutral?

Race 10: Finding Adventure

Why do you think that is happening?

What do you need to do to move forward there?

Where do you see the most movement so far?

Why do you think you made a lot of progress in each category?

How will you celebrate your victories?

This is only the beginning. You have just completed 10 races and are on track to reclaim the life you desire. **Celebrate!**

I am always changing racetracks and changing cars, along with working on my mind and body. We are all a work in progress, and you may want to stop by and have a look around at this workbook again and again. You are always welcome here, visit as often as you need to, and continue to change course and live your best life!

Keep your pedal to the metal and don't let anything stop you. **You are worth it!**

Appendix I: The Change Course Assessment

The following assessment is intended to help you determine what stage you are at in your journey of healing and change. This assessment will measure five components that are essential to changing course in your personal race toward a happier life:

1. **Change** – A willing heart is half the battle. This component measures how willing you are to change.

2. **Self** – This component measures the health of your self-esteem as well as your acceptance of who you are today.

3. **Risk** – This component measures how willing you are to take risks.

4. **Energy** – This component measures how well you are managing your vitality and health.

5. **Healing** – This component measures your current progress on healing the hurts and loss that may be holding you back from the life you want.

In order to track your progress, you may want to use a separate sheet of paper to take this same assessment at the start; then again halfway point of this journey, and finally at the end (or a year later). Recognizing and celebrating progress is an important part of living a life you love.

Answer the following questions to the best of your ability. Don't overthink it; just circle the first answer that comes to mind.

Reclaim Control of Your Life Workbook

1. I struggle to break bad habits.

    a. Never   b. Rarely   c. Sometimes   d. Frequently   e. Always

2. I get really nervous when I'm about to make any changes in my life.

    a. Never   b. Rarely   c. Sometimes   d. Frequently   e. Always

3. I intentionally make positive improvements in my life on a regular basis.

    a. Never   b. Rarely   c. Sometimes   d. Frequently   e. Always

4. I get frustrated when I alter my regular routines.

    a. Never   b. Rarely   c. Sometimes   d. Frequently   e. Always

5. I know I need to make changes in my life, but struggle to start.

    a. Never   b. Rarely   c. Sometimes   d. Frequently   e. Always

6. I like the person I am today.

    a. Never   b. Rarely   c. Sometimes   d. Frequently   e. Always

7. I spend time and energy pleasing others and making them happy.

    a. Never   b. Rarely   c. Sometimes   d. Frequently   e. Always

Appendix I: The Change Course Assessment

8. I have people in my life who believe in me.

    a. Never   b. Rarely   c. Sometimes   d. Frequently   e. Always

9. Things that people teased and/or criticized me about still bother me today.

    a. Never   b. Rarely   c. Sometimes   d. Frequently   e. Always

10. I believe I am uniquely and beautifully created by God.

    a. Never   b. Rarely   c. Sometimes   d. Frequently   e. Always

11. Fear of failing stops me from trying something new.

    a. Never   b. Rarely   c. Sometimes   d. Frequently   e. Always

12. When I fail at something, I try again another way.

    a. Never   b. Rarely   c. Sometimes   d. Frequently   e. Always

13. I spend a lot of time analyzing new opportunities before taking action.

    a. Never   b. Rarely   c. Sometimes   d. Frequently   e. Always

14. I like to try new things.

    a. Never   b. Rarely   c. Sometimes   d. Frequently   e. Always

15. I like to live a life of adventure, even if it doesn't go as planned.

      a. Never   b. Rarely   c. Sometimes   d. Frequently   e. Always

16. I intentionally take time to relax.

      a. Never   b. Rarely   c. Sometimes   d. Frequently   e. Always

17. I get enough sleep on a regular basis.

      a. Never   b. Rarely   c. Sometimes   d. Frequently   e. Always

18. I make food choices that fuel my body in a healthy way.

      a. Never   b. Rarely   c. Sometimes   d. Frequently   e. Always

19. I move my body with exercise.

      a. Never   b. Rarely   c. Sometimes   d. Frequently   e. Always

20. I make sure my schedule includes doing things I enjoy.

      a. Never   b. Rarely   c. Sometimes   d. Frequently   e. Always

21. I feel stuck in grief over the losses I've experienced in my life.

      a. Never   b. Rarely   c. Sometimes   d. Frequently   e. Always

Appendix I: The Change Course Assessment

22. I feel like past trauma is holding me back from the life I want.

    a. Never   b. Rarely   c. Sometimes   d. Frequently   e. Always

23. I engage in addictive behaviors that help me escape my life or numb the pain I feel.

    a. Never   b. Rarely   c. Sometimes   d. Frequently   e. Always

24. I spend multiple hours each week thinking about childhood trauma that still affects me today.

    a. Never   b. Rarely   c. Sometimes   d. Frequently   e. Always

25. I am drawn to partners or friends that make me feel inferior.

    a. Never   b. Rarely   c. Sometimes   d. Frequently   e. Always

Evaluation

Circle the letter of your selected answer for the question number indicated. Add the column totals using the corresponding score amounts of each. Add all of the columns together and enter your total score in the blank below the box.

CHANGE

Question Number					
1	a = 5 points	b = 4 points	c = 3 points	d = 2 points	e = 1 point
2	a = 5 points	b = 4 points	c = 3 points	d = 2 points	e = 1 point
3	a = 1 point	b = 2 points	c = 3 points	d = 4 points	e = 5 points
4	a = 5 points	b = 4 points	c = 3 points	d = 2 points	e = 1 point
5	a = 5 points	b = 4 points	c = 3 points	d = 2 points	e = 1 point
Column Total					

My CHANGE score today: _____

My CHANGE score at half way point: _____

My CHANGE score at follow-up: _____

Appendix I: The Change Course Assessment

SELF

Question Number					
6	a = 1 point	b = 2 points	c = 3 points	d = 4 points	e = 5 points
7	a = 5 points	b = 4 points	c = 3 points	d = 2 points	e = 1 point
8	a = 1 point	b = 2 points	c = 3 points	d = 4 points	e = 5 points
9	a = 5 points	b = 4 points	c = 3 points	d = 2 points	e = 1 point
10	a = 1 point	b = 2 points	c = 3 points	d = 4 points	e = 5 points
Column Total					

My SELF score today: _____

My SELF score at half way point: _____

My SELF score at follow-up: _____

RISK

Question Number					
11	a = 5 points	b = 4 points	c = 3 points	d = 2 points	e = 1 point
12	a = 1 point	b = 2 points	c = 3 points	d = 4 points	e = 5 points
13	a = 5 points	b = 4 points	c = 3 points	d = 2 points	e = 1 point
14	a = 1 point	b = 2 points	c = 3 points	d = 4 points	e = 5 points
15	a = 1 point	b = 2 points	c = 3 points	d = 4 points	e = 5 points
Column Total					

My RISK score today: _____

My RISK score at half way point: _____

My RISK score at follow-up: _____

Appendix I: The Change Course Assessment

ENERGY

Question Number					
16	a = 1 point	b = 2 points	c = 3 points	d = 4 points	e = 5 points
17	a = 1 point	b = 2 points	c = 3 points	= 4 points	e = 5 points
18	a = 1 point	b = 2 points	c = 3 points	d = 4 points	e = 5 points
19	a = 1 point	b = 2 points	c = 3 points	d = 4 points	e = 5 points
20	a = 1 point	b = 2 points	c = 3 points	d = 4 points	e = 5 points
Column Total					

My ENERGY score today: _____

My ENERGY score at half way point: _____

My ENERGY score at follow-up: _____

HEALING

Question Number					
21	a = 5 point	b = 4 points	c = 3 points	d = 2 points	e = 1 point
22	a = 5 points	b = 4 points	c = 3 points	d = 2 points	e = 1 point
23	a = 5 points	b = 4 points	c = 3 points	d = 2 points	e = 1 point
24	a = 5 points	b = 4 points	c = 3 points	d = 2 points	e = 1 point
25	a = 5 points	b = 4 points	c = 3 points	d = 2 points	e = 1 point
Column Total					

My HEALING score today: _____

My HEALING score at half way point: _____

My HEALING score at follow-up: _____

Appendix I: The Change Course Assessment

CHART YOUR COURSE

Chart your scores (now, at your Half Way point, and at Follow up later) on the line graphs below by marking your total score for each category. Then read about your finding and racing tips in the next section.

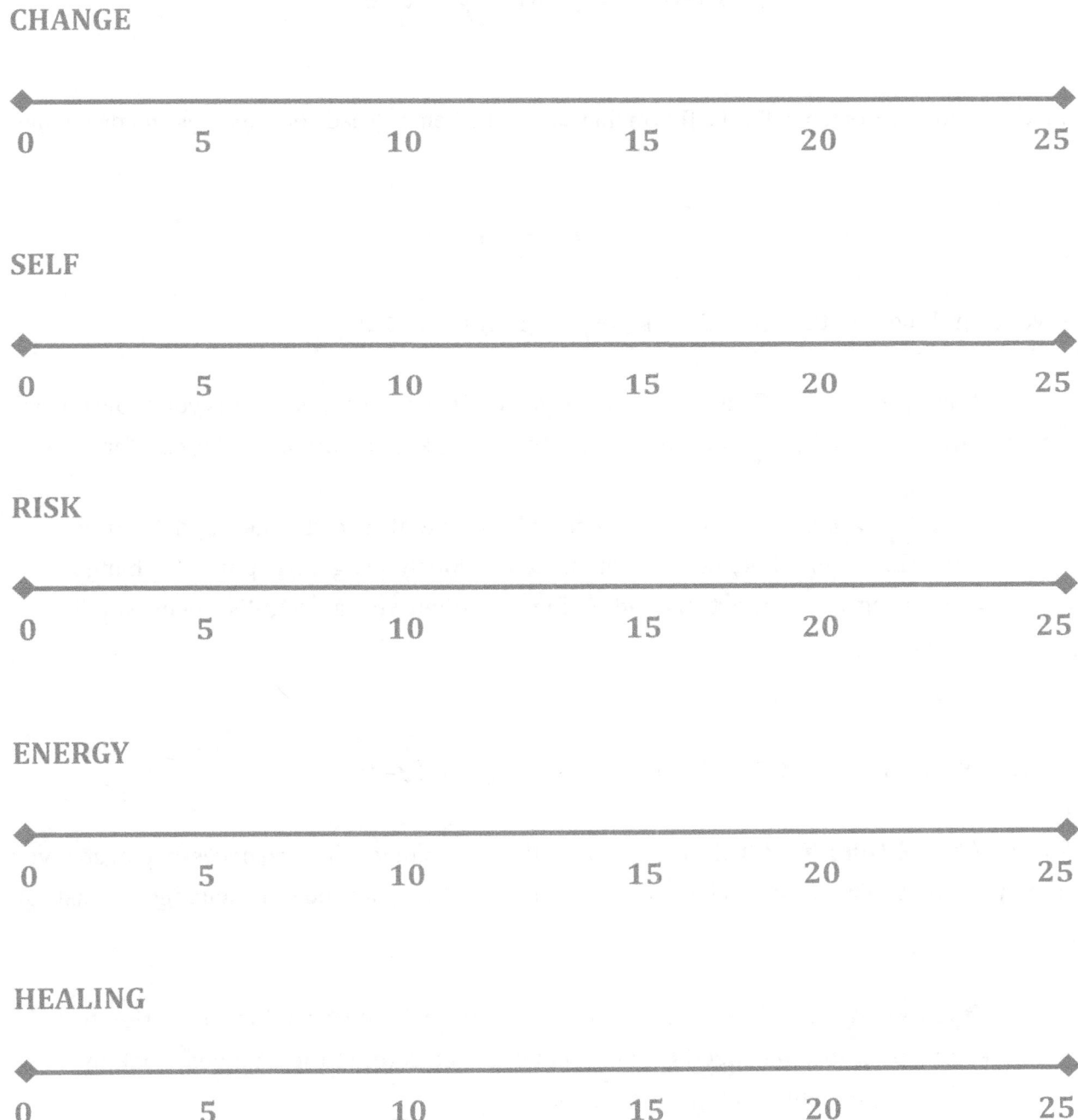

Change Course Assessment Findings and Racing Tips

Find your total score range for the five racing categories below. Read your findings and racing tips.

CHANGE

If your total score in the CHANGE category is a range of **5–12**:

You are Change **Resistant**. This doesn't mean you can't change; it just means you typically will avoid change, especially the hard kind of change that takes you outside your comfort zone.

Racing Tips: Set your mind to be willing to embrace change opportunities when they come. Take note of when you are "pushing against" possible change and opting for comfort instead. Celebrate when you accomplish even small changes.

If your total score in the CHANGE category is a range of **13–19**:

You are Change **Compliant**. This means you will make changes that are necessary, even if you don't want to. You're willing to be uncomfortable for a time, but too much change too fast can wear you out.

Racing Tips: Make sure to keep your "why" in front of you for motivation to keep going. You may need to take frequent breaks to let the changes "soak in" before implementing the next change.

Appendix I: The Change Course Assessment

If your total score in the CHANGE category is a range of **20–25:**

You are a Change **Master**. Not only do you like change, you thrive on it. In fact, sometimes you'll make changes just because you're bored and need some change to keep things exciting.

> *Racing Tips:* Make sure the changes you are making are the right ones. Enjoy the journey along the way more than the destination.

SELF

If your total score in the SELF category is a range of **5–12:**

Your SELF IMAGE tank is *low*. You have a negative image of yourself, and your self-acceptance needs more fuel. Don't worry, we'll work on that throughout this workbook. If you do the work, you'll begin to see yourself for the amazing person you are!

> *Racing Tips:* Watch out for negative self-talk. It can cause damage to your self-image. Keep "flipping the script" on those negative thoughts to re-fuel. Celebrate when you accomplish even small changes throughout this journey.

If your total score in the SELF category is a range of **13–19:**
Your SELF IMAGE tank is *½ to ¾ full*. You've done some work on your self-image and have made a lot of progress. Good job! Some days you have great self-image, but then other days you don't.

> *Racing Tips:* Do the exercises in each chapter to keep filling your "self" tank. Watch out for negative self-talk and make sure to hang up on the past when it comes calling.

If your total score in the SELF category is a range of **20–25:**

Your SELF IMAGE tank is *full*. Good job! It looks like you have a healthy self-image, and you understand the value of self-acceptance.

> *Racing Tips:* Keep filling your tank with the good stuff you've done in the past to get to where you are today. You can be a great help to others who need to fill their "self" tank.

RISK

If your total score in the RISK category is a range of **5–12:**

You are Risk *Averse*. This means when there's a risk involved in change, you'll run the other way. Past failures have made you leery to try again, you likely perceive you'll run the risk of failing again.

> *Racing Tips:* Start telling yourself that with risk, comes rewards. One of the rewards is learning from both our failures and our successes. Figure out what you are supposed to learn from mistakes and disappointments. Celebrate the small changes you make every time. Focus on the rewards!

If your total score in the RISK category is a range of **13-19:**

You are Risk *Neutral*. You're not opposed to taking risks, but they need to be the right risks for you to go forward. If there's too much on the line, you might not make the change that's needed.

> *Racing Tips:* Remember that if you try and fail at something, you can always try again and take a different approach.

Appendix I: The Change Course Assessment

If your total score in the RISK category is a range of **20-25:**

You are a Risk **Thriver**. You have learned taking healthy risks opens your world to new possibilities and develops your self-confidence as you meet new people and challenges. When you have had failures, you've pivoted and tried again.

> *Racing Tips:* Make sure the risks you take lead you to the life you want to live. Don't take risks that will detour you from what you want most.

ENERGY

If your total score in the ENERGY category is a range of **5-12:**

Your ENERGY level is **low**. However, this isn't a surprise to you. You feel your lack of energy every day. For whatever reason, you haven't been tending to your own self enough. But that all stops today! (Note to parents and caregivers: You need to have energy to be able to help others. This may seem obvious, but we tend to forget self-care when life gets busy.)

> *Racing Tips:* Start small. Do one small thing every day to start raising your energy level. Go to bed 30 minutes earlier or drink an extra glass of water. Read a book for 15 minutes or take a long bubble bath one night a week. Even small things can give our energy levels a boost.

If your total score in the ENERGY category is a range of **13–19:**

Your ENERGY level is **medium**. In some areas of your life you are not consistently keeping your energy levels up.

> *Racing Tips:* Look at where you are doing things well and then consistently do more of those things (self-care, sleep, exercise, better food choices).

If your total score in the ENERGY category is a range of **20–25:**

Your ENERGY level is **high**. Good job You understand the value of taking care of your health and vitality. You know you need energy for the life you want to live.

Racing Tips: Keep your levels up, and make sure you don't overdo it by obsessing and making it your primary focus. Celebrate your success and continue to do what is working for you.

HEALING

If your total score in the HEALING category is a range of **5–12:**

Your HEALING needs **help**. This is why you are here, and why you chose to start this race to change course. Good for you! You haven't been able to dig in and do the type of healing work that is required. This workbook will help you get started down that path.

Racing Tips: Be patient with yourself. Healing work is hard, but the results are amazing! Be willing to face the hard stuff and celebrate your small steps forward.

If your total Score in the HEALING category is a range of **13–19:**

Your HEALING needs **momentum**. It looks like you've engaged in healing work, but you have more to do. That's okay! This workbook is full of opportunities to get your healing work rolling again.

Racing Tips: Since you've made some healing progress in your life, you know it's not always easy. Make sure you take small steps—and always celebrate your victories.

Appendix I: The Change Course Assessment

If your total score in the HEALING category is a range of **20–25**:

Your HEALING needs ***more healing***. Good job so far! You've done a lot of healing work, but you aren't finished yet. Our bodies tend to always need some type of healing work. For every place we find healing, we find other places that also need healing.

> *Racing Tips:* Be willing to dig into new areas and new levels of healing. Healing helps us to change course and live the life we want. Never stop doing the work and celebrating your victories.

Now that you know more about where you are at in your race to change course, you are ready to finish preparing to race. Go back to the section you read last, and then keep going. If you have completed the Assessment Evaluation at your Follow Up point, continue reading and celebrate your accomplishment!

The Road Ahead

I hope and pray this workbook was a blessing to you and brought you closer to your heavenly father as you navigated towards your purpose and regained control. May you feel God's loving spirit envelop you with His love.

Even though we have made progress, life will continue to be challenging for us as it strengthens and stretches us. When I have difficulty staying on course I read my anchor verse. It can be found in John 13:34 NIV. Jesus tells us:

> *"A new command I give you: Love one another.*
> *As I have loved you, so you must love one another."*

What is your anchor verse? What will keep you on track?

I would love to hear from you!
E-mail me at: Leslie@LadyRacing.com
www.LadyRacing.com

Leader Guide

If you have decided to lead a team of racers to the finish line using this workbook, I would like to offer a few suggestions.

As the leader you may feel inclined to tell them what they should do. I encourage you to guide them instead so they can find what works best for them. Motivate and rally them to stay on track as they navigate through the Change Course Workbook. You will be taking your racers through each chapter and allowing them to complete the exercises. You will facilitate conversations between the racers and lovingly guide them along by using the questions to aid them in coming up with their own answers.

Setting the Rules of the Race

As the leader, it will be your job to set the rules of the race. These are the expectations for the group. Here are some of the rules I recommend putting in place:

- Be Punctual–Meetings will start and end on time.

- Be Confidential–This is a safe place to share. Racers can share as much or as little as they like, but everything said here, stays here. If someone prefers not to share, suggest they say, "I'll pass this time."

- Don't FIX–Refrain from giving unsolicited advice to your fellow racers. Avoid judging statements like: "You should…", or "If it were me, I'd…"

- Speak for Yourself–Use "I" statements instead of general statements when sharing.

- Be Prepared–Each racer must complete their exercises prior to the meeting. Let your racers know what you expect them to do.

- Be Respectful–Each racer needs the opportunity to share. Be mindful of your time so everyone has a chance to share. (Divide the amount of total time allotted for sharing by the amount of people in your group to determine how much time each racer will be given.)

Add any other "rules" as they pertain to your group and the structure of your meetings.

Preparing to Guide Your Racers

As the leader of a group, your preparation is essential to the success of your racers to change course. Here are some tips that can help you:

- Prerequisite: Read the Change Course: One Lady's Race from Acceptance to Adventure chapter from the book and work through the corresponding exercises in the workbook prior to meeting with your group. Being familiar with the material will equip you to facilitate the session.

- Set up your meeting room in a circle, horseshoe or square/rectangle if possible, to allow for an intimate setting ideal for participants the leader to view and hear each other.

- Arrive 15 minutes early to greet your group members as they arrive.

- When it's appropriate to do so, share your own story, and be vulnerable with your struggles. This will give the racers permission to do the same. This doesn't make you the expert; it makes you authentic as the leader. We all are a "work-in-progress."

- If your group is larger, you may want to break into smaller groups for discussion time with instructions for the discussion.

- Respect where everyone is at in their faith journey. Don't push your beliefs on the racers, but rather guide them to explore their beliefs. Racers don't have to agree with each other's beliefs to learn from each other, but they do need to respect others.

Facilitating the Exercises

Each race (chapter) in this workbook contains a theme that goes along with the chapter in *Change Course*. The premise is to help others envision their own story as they read the author's. Each exercise is designed to help them do just that. The exercises vary in length and number depending on the chapter theme. Each chapter contains the same "Five Race Exercises" to help the racers reflect on the exercises they completed.

As the leader, you can choose to highlight one of the exercises for the discussion and sharing time, or simply use the "Five Race Exercises" as your discussion points. It depends on the dynamics of your group and the purpose for your meeting time together.

Here are some tips to help you as you facilitate each session:

- Ask open-ended questions that require more than a yes or no answer.

- Instead of answering your own questions when no one speaks up, instead try re-phrasing a question.

- Encourage others to answer the same question.

- Be affirming by thanking people for sharing and contributing to the discussion.

- Keep the discussion on topic.

- Instead of rejecting an answer as wrong, ask for more information, or how they arrived at that decision.

- Stop racers who try to "fix" other racers. Guide the conversation back to the person sharing.

Follow up after the Finish Line

Plan how you will follow up after the racers have finished the course. This will help the racers continue to change course and live the life they want. Here are some examples of follow-up options:

- Reconvene the Group–Host a follow-up meeting two to three months after the end of your race together. Use this as a touch point for accountability on their goals.

- Schedule a 1:1–if you prefer to make it more personal, schedule individual follow-up meetings monthly following the end of your race together.

- Group Chat–create a private group on social media or start a chat room where everyone can share progress on their continued racing efforts.

- Follow up–as you near the end of your course, ask your racers how they would like to follow up after the race is finished.

Acknowledgments

Thank you God, my Heavenly Father, who guides me daily.

Special thanks to my beta readers and workshops attendees who gave me feedback on what works and what needed to change course. You always gave great answers, and I am thankful for our time together.

Thanks to my husband Jim for putting up with me. I am a handful, but he was always patient and kind listening to my endless prattling on about how this workbook should evolve—and then not saying anything when I changed my mind and went a different direction.

Many people gave of their precious knowledge and love to make this workbook a reality. I will never be able to thank enough, Mina Carlson and Tenaya (T.J.) Tison, two of the most skilled and God-filled people I know. Also, to my editors Connie Anderson and Judy Brenner, thank you for your expertise in making this workbook readable. The beauty of this book is because Lacey Ballard is an amazing artist and Sue Stein is fabulous at creating the interior design of books. Thank you everyone for making this workbook the best it could possibly be.

www.ingramcontent.com/pod-product-compliance
Lightning Source LLC
Chambersburg PA
CBHW081230080526
44587CB00022B/3882